A Murmuration

David Cooke was born in the UK but his family comes from the West of Ireland. He won a Gregory Award in 1977, while still an undergraduate at Nottingham University. His retrospective collection, *In the Distance*, was published in 2011 by Night Publishing. A new collection, *Work Horses*, was published by Ward Wood in 2012. His poems, translations and reviews have appeared widely in the UK, Ireland and beyond in journals such as *Agenda*, *Ambit*, *The Cortland Review*, *The Interpreter's House*, *The Irish Press*, *The London Magazine*, *Magma*, *The Morning Star*, *New Walk*, *The North*, *Poetry Ireland Review*, *Poetry Salzburg Review*, *The Reader*, *The SHOp* and *Stand*. Married with four grown-up children, he was for many years the Head of Modern Languages at a large comprehensive school in Cleethorpes. More recently, he has earned his living as an internet bookseller, but is now happily retired.

Also by Two Rivers Poets:
David Attwooll, *The Sound Ladder* (2015)
Paul Bavister, *Miletree* (1996)
Paul Bavister, *Glass* (1998)
Paul Bavister, *The Prawn Season* (2002)
Adrian Blamires, *The Effect of Coastal Processes* (2005)
Adrian Blamires, *The Pang Valley* (2010)
Adrian Blamires & Peter Robinson (eds.), *The Arts of Peace* (2014)
Joseph Butler, *Hearthstone* (2006)
Terry Cree, *Fruit* (2014)
Jane Draycott and Lesley Saunders, *Christina the Astonishing* (1998)
Jane Draycott, *Tideway* (2002)
John Froy, *Eggshell: A Decorator's Notes* (2007)
David Greenslade, *Zeus Amoeba* (2009)
A. F. Harrold, *Logic and the Heart* (2004)
A. F. Harrold, *Flood* (2009)
A. F. Harrold, *The Point of Inconvenience* (2013)
Ian House, *Cutting the Quick* (2005)
Ian House, *Nothing's Lost* (2014)
Gill Learner, *The Agister's Experiment* (2011)
Kate Noakes, *The Wall Menders* (2009)
Victoria Pugh, *Mrs Marvellous* (2008)
Peter Robinson, *English Nettles and Other Poems* (2010)
Peter Robinson (ed.), *Reading Poetry: An Anthology* (2011)
Peter Robinson (ed.), *A Mutual Friend: Poems for Charles Dickens* (2012)
Peter Robinson, *Foreigners, Drunks and Babies: Eleven Stories* (2013)
Lesley Saunders, *Her Leafy Eye* (2009)
Lesley Saunders, *Cloud Camera* (2012)
Susan Utting, *Houses Without Walls* (2006)
Susan Utting, *Fair's Fair* (2012)

A Murmuration

David Cooke

First published in the UK in 2015 by Two Rivers Press
7 Denmark Road, Reading RG1 5PA.
www.tworiverspress.com

© David Cooke 2015

The right of the poet to be identified as the author of the work
has been asserted by him in accordance with the Copyright,
Designs and Patents Act of 1988.

All rights reserved. No part of this publication may be reproduced,
stored in or introduced into a retrieval system, or transmitted,
in any form, or by any means (electronic, mechanical, photocopying,
recording or otherwise) without the prior written permission of
the publisher.

ISBN 978-1-909747-11-1

1 2 3 4 5 6 7 8 9

Two Rivers Press is represented in the UK by Inpress Ltd
and distributed by Central Books.

Cover design and illustration by Sally Castle
Text design by Nadja Guggi and typeset in Janson and Parisine

Printed and bound in Great Britain by Imprint Digital, Exeter.

For my children

Daniel, James, Anna & Helen

Acknowledgements

I take the opportunity to thank the editors of the following where these poems have previously appeared: *Agenda*, *Ambit*, *And Other Poems*, *Antiphon*, *Ariadne's Thread*, BODY (Czech Republic), *The Bow Wow Shop*, *Cake*, *Cannon's Mouth*, *Carillon*, *The Dock*, *Dream Catcher*, *Fourteen*, *Kumquat*, *London Magazine*, *Magma*, *Message in a Bottle*, *My Delayed Reactions*, *New Walk*, *Ole' Chanty*, *Orbis*, *Pennine Platform*, *Poetry and Audience*, *Poetry Salzburg Review*, *Pop Up Poetry 2014*, *Prole*, *The Screech Owl*, *Seventh Quarry*, *Stachtes* (Greece), *Stand*, *The Stare's Nest*, *The Undertow Review*, *The Wilderness House Review* (USA) and *Yareah* (USA).

The following are revised versions of poems which first appeared in *Brueghel's Dancers* (published by Free Man's Press Editions, 1984): 'An Anniversary', 'Travelling Back', 'The Pasternak Season', 'August Schleicher' and 'The Hunters in the Snow'.

'A Northern Resort' was broadcast by Radio Humberside on 3 December 2010 in their series *Larkin About; A poetic tribute*. An earlier version of 'The Ice House' was reprinted in *Versions of the North* (edited by Ian Parks for Five Leaves Publications, 2013.) 'An Anniversary' and 'The Burghers of Calais' were reprinted in the anthology *Poets in Person* (edited by Aprilia Zank for Indigo Dreams Publishing, 2014.)

Finally, I would like to thank Anders Dahlgren for reprinting my poems about Malta on his website *Mediterranean Poetry* (Sweden) and the student editors of *Reading University Creative Arts Anthologies* (2011 to 2013).

Contents

At Woody's Top | 3

I. Before the Storm

The Ice House | 7
The Burghers of Calais | 8
Before the Storm | 9
After Bruegel | 10
Faro | 12
An Anniversary | 13
Travelling Back | 14
The Pasternak Season | 15
The Morning of the World | 16
The Manor House at Alford | 18
The Railway House | 19
Canal | 20
Cities | 22
Distances | 23
A Writer's Retreat | 24
National Trust | 25

II. The Sleeping Lady of Malta

The Sleeping Lady of Malta | 29
Valetta | 30
Prickly Pear | 31
Mdina | 32
Malti | 33
Maltese Buses | 34

III. When Smokey Sings

Bookshop | 39
When Smokey Sings | 40
Stepping Out | 41
Gasometers | 42
Oscar Wilde Walk, Reading | 43
For Antoinette | 44

IV. A Murmuration

A Murmuration | 49
A Northern Resort | 50
The Owls of Cleethorpes | 51
To the Lighthouse | 52
Koala | 53
Leaving St. Kilda | 54
Ontology | 55
Stéphane Mallarmé | 56
Sea Breeze | 57
August Schleicher | 58
The Swan | 59
The Pheasant | 60
The Hunters in the Snow | 62

... a murmuration of starlings

rising in joy over wolds ...

W.H. Auden

At Woody's Top

Trying to see it, I look across a landscape
on the raised edge of Lincolnshire,
whose flat productive acres have wrinkled
into the rise and dip
of the Wolds, as if geology
had assumed a rhythm like verse.

And though it's all a question
of pressure and upheavals,
and the slow relentless stroke of weather,
my gaze settles on a view
that has the fixity
and composure of a final draft.

Beyond the mizzling bluster
of a late October morning
the distances are sealed in silence,
where gulls flicker above the copse
like random thoughts
that may or may not amount to something.

I. Before the Storm

The Ice House

Imagine stepping from endless
summer into that compact
lifeless core; and the way you'd
stoop to gain some purchase
with your pick and spade,

leaning again into a harvest
of sullen, grainy crystal –
its dead leaves, dead seeds and insects;
then savouring its squelch and give,
its rasping slither into pails.

Lugged across that sweep of lawns
and past the lightsome gestures
of their pagan sculpture,
it is let down with a breathless
grunt onto the pantry floor.

In a room where all is brightness
they are laying out fresh linen;
will adjust to the nth degree
of seemliness a table fit for quality –
the talented mistress of their king.

The Burghers of Calais

after Auguste Rodin

Connoisseurs of the smart move,
appraising the prices of commodities
and men, they stepped up against
their instincts, their futures anchored
in marriageable daughters,
the grit and astuteness of sons.

Their acquisitive eyes had once
been lit by the weight in tapestries
from Bruges or Ghent, the patience
entwined in filigree work or lace.
Their solid tables sustained them.

Stripped here to a stark decency,
they are each wearing a halter
as they shuffle beyond
the starved confines of town.

Seeming defiant, one has stopped;
another cowers behind him.
Without recourse, all are abject –
bound in the fellowship of those
reaching beyond their fear.

Before the Storm

At no age at all you've started to feel
how a life gets mired in memories,
the way each backward glance
is like a noose that tightens.

Across flat *versts* of muddled terrain
your distant city glimmers –
reduced to a few bright rooms
where you were first indulged

and then became accomplished –
working through grammars
and the language of flowers,
your music opened

at some tricksy *bagatelle*.
Each week the house would echo
to the rites of the samovar,
the clack of heels on a floor ...

But in this straggling barracks town
which you must now endure,
accepting the slavishness
of the overlooked, the weary,

you hear at night the cries of wolves
through birches, can sense
their luminous eyes,
their restless, circling hunger.

After Bruegel

The magpie on the gallows
has seen it all, but now
remembers nothing;

the bright beads
of his eyes swivelling
remorselessly

from one catastrophe
to another. And this
is what, so far,

has kept him alive
as he hops to a roadkill,
or swoops next

to a glut of carnage
in quiet fields where mist
has smothered

whisps of smoke,
the faint groans of horse
or trampled pikeman.

Untroubled by claims
that dynasties make,
he senses vaguely

that life is good,
as they do also
who dance beneath him,

their day's work done,
seizing the moment
in a loose circle

of movement and song.
Uninvolved and unthreatened
the scavenger spares them

his briefest glance
before returning
to that wider view

of the valley
and mountains
his lofty perch affords him,

who soon will stretch
his wings and then,
unnoticed, sail away.

Faro

We're two hours' flight from a northern spring;
the impassive sky we've left behind us
a canvas primed but still awaiting
some splash of inspiration;

the grey pavements underscoring
routines we cling to; but here,
our touchdown lights a spark in a town
whose name suggests a beacon

and where all winter, unknown to us,
the orange trees on the *Largo da Sé*
ripened slowly, revealing now
a constellation of sweetness on a coast

whose warmth detains the storks
that headed once for Africa;
and as if plonked recklessly
on rooftops, ledges, hoardings,

their nests rise from platforms
of branches, twigs and rags,
growing bulkier year by year –
ancestral homes they sublet to sparrows.

But when we get too close, climbing
the bell tower, we find ourselves
in a perfect storm of beak
and wings like loose-rigged sails.

An Anniversary

Famous only for Rousseau's dreamy sojourn,
Chambéry lay huddled at the foot
of its calendar landscape, and there it was
we met, as if compelled
by a pattern in the lines on a map
to inhabit that region of mountains.

I wonder now do you still recall
our romantic isolation: how we grew familiar
with narrow streets so reticent and formal,
kept tidy as their own concerns –
cramped shops replete with goods
for a bustling clientele.

All that legendary summer we spent
our afternoons on the slopes
of St. Michel and made love
in a shimmering absence –
only the insects adrift in silence,
the gliders above at a decent height.

Travelling Back

I take a train and put your face
behind me, settling back into rhythm
as smartly the wheels gain speed,
then haul across the counties.

Not wanting to read, I try
till suddenly distracted –
my own intangible features
afloat like a wraith in glass

beyond which dissolving
fields become a haunt
for predators, a world of tiny
imperceptible shrieks ...

Above the merging trees
the evening's light is wasting.
Pawning our time,
again I'll make it pay.

The Pasternak Season

All last night the snow
was falling and has quietly
drowned the gardens.
A tasteless manna
that settles to fill
the morning, it redefines
the starkness of trees,
properties the day
with stillness and light.

The changed air outside
will blade your ears
when you broach it,
as expectation leaves
its prints in snow.

The Morning of the World

Jules Supervielle

All around arose a thousand noises,
yet still so filled with silences
that the ear seemed attuned
to the song of its innocence.

All things alive and self-absorbed,
the neighbourhood was a mirror
in which creation moved,
entranced, toward fulfilment.

The palm trees, finding a form
in which to sway with pure delight,
summoned distant birds
to show them their leafwork.

A white horse encountered Man
advancing quietly, while the Earth
revolved around him, inspiring
his astrological heart.

The horse twitched its nostrils
and whinnied as if in flight.
Lost in its dream time
the creature galloped away.

On streets where children
and women seemed adrift like clouds,
they came together to find their souls,
moving from shadows to light.

A thousand roosters crowed,
mapping out the landscape,
the ocean waves hesitant
between twenty landfalls.

The hour so rich in oarsmen
and phosphorescent mermaids,
the stars overlooked their images
in those speaking waters.

The Manor House at Alford

Finding his feet on the right side of history,
some notable, a name, acquired this house,
when he laid new money down for impeccable
brickwork and the chamfered beams

upholding its fireplace, the ceilings,
a world; and blithely assuming
what may have seemed the burdens
of stewardship, his life was well appointed.

From dawn till dusk, and by degree,
days creaked on cogs and wheels like the lift
in which his wife ascended. Hutched in the attic,
his servants' lives were entangled in bells.

While their descendants, freer now
and more uncertain, can pay to view
the relics of each sanitized era,
glimpsing here through perspex

the insides of walls whose handsomeness
was all a fascia, a blind, across
an arcane structure whose ties could not hold.
Slowly the house disassembled itself,

becoming a sump for wealth
in deferential twilight, as lost trades
and the skills of mechanicals
were reinvented to claim a premium.

And if we're now unsure who owns it,
trustees are tasked to make it pay –
its garden reduced to raggedy box,
a few late windfalls, pecked at, abandoned.

The Railway House

for Greg Freeman

If I were to own it, this foursquare,
solid house, I'd fix a plaque
with a single word: *Fortitude*
to show the way it holds its own
between two streets
and the urban clearway.

From an upstairs window
I'd slip through time, imagining
the features of fish-dock lumpers,
their pale-faced kids and wives,
sliding past on rails
to freedom and the Wolds.

As in some genre painting,
I'd sense the innocence
with which they grasp new-fangled days –
their faith in clockwork, uniforms,
the black and white
of *Bradshaw's Guides*,

leaving behind them
a trackless pathway that rises up
on brambled banks, the abandoned
corridor prowled by foxes
above which kestrels hover,
eyeing their chances.

Canal

for Ken Head

From the dead end of a side street
in a shuffling market town
I follow the abandoned canal,
enticed by the promise

of glimpses into secretive lives –
the otters, voles, and occasional
migrants whose images feature
on the information panel.

With an earlier start and clearer sky
I might have reached the sea
across twelve open miles
where the Wolds have levelled;

but dither, first, at the edge
of the water with barely feral
coots and ducks. Risking the rain,
I move on beneath darkened trees

past the sandbagged thresholds
of a new-build estate; and then,
beyond it, the cluttered outpost
of the reclamation yard.

A first generation towny,
with an afternoon to kill, I keep
pace with sluggish water, its channel
constricted by banks of growth

whose headstrong pinks
and yellows tumble down
to silted shallows, where trailing
branches dowse their leaves.

Determined, later, to look up
its history, I find it hard
to picture its heyday, or guess
how long it served a purpose

in these quiet fields, where
a slow-moving herd pays me
no mind and keeps no memory
of softly spoken Culchies

who muttered wryly
into drink and flopped down,
exhausted, in a kip on Irish Hill,
a street the locals named for them.

Cities

There's another city inside the city. It lays
its template of odours across postal districts.

One day, perhaps, you'll sense it
beneath your speed: a faint hint of fox piss

that clings to street lamps and bollards.
Leaving its marker, it establishes different laws.

Below our fences there are badger setts
and mole runs, scrabbling polities

obscured by codes, dissimulation, the plunge
of adits into the dark of the earth.

It's 5 a.m. and a rackety slew of birdcalls
fills in a gap between late revels and early shifts.

All day the city accumulates heat, hatching
prematurely the high rise predators.

In a colour supplement once I read
about Year Zero in a city called Phnomh Penh

and how the jungle broke it up
when all its people had marched away.

Distances

Philippe Jaccottet

In the high air the swifts are circling.
Higher still the invisible stars
are circling too. Let day withdraw
to the earth's limits, those fires
will reappear above a stretch
of dark sand.
              And so we inhabit
a world of distances, of movement,
where the heart is drawn
from the tree to the bird, from birds
to distant stars, and from the stars
returns to its own affections.
Thus love, in a shuttered house,
increases, a servant to the careworn,
holding a lamp in its hand.

A Writer's Retreat

for Paul Sutherland

To the tree-framed haven
of Woody's Top
in Lincolnshire we come
by separate ways
to find ourselves
in language:
devotees of syntax
and syllable
who map out the confines
of our writers' hideaway,
reinventing a space
for contemplation
and brisk walks,
each of us a citizen
of an imagined
Peredelkino –
free to interpret
shifts in the weather
and the auguries of birds
whose flights with luck
we'll fledge
anew in words.

National Trust

Floor by floor we learn
their histories: upstairs downstairs
knowing their places.

Above our cream teas –
the baby bats fine-tuning
echolocation.

II. The Sleeping Lady of Malta

The Sleeping Lady of Malta

Before these islands acquired their history,
a mythology of creeds and sieges,
there was a dream of flesh in stone –

Let's call her *Melitensis*,
handsome as only a woman might be
who lies at ease with ampleness.

Her children are scattered;
her days a pampered twilight –
until at length she floats away

beyond the ruins of temples,
beyond disfigurement and urban sprawl,
to reach the furthest island,

a stepping stone to where
each day the light comes good
that paints her lemony limestone dwelling

and where the air
in the evening is a distillation of herbs
and unfamiliar flowers.

Valetta

High on its promontory the Grand Master's city
seems to be carved from living rock;
its curtain walls rising from undressed sandstone
that heaves them clear of water.

Secured against past enemies,
their wind-scoured surfaces are embattled
against mere blow-ins: the indigent shrubs
and bushes that cling improbably to crevices

in a wilderness of hewn stone –
the riddled maze of limestone blocks
where lizards and heat-crazed insects
pursue inscrutable wars.

Etched on sky that's buffed
by a soft drift of cloud, the finer detail dazzles –
the teetering balconies of citizens,
the arcaded gardens, where visitors share

in a view across the harbour
drawing its line against unruly surges,
its creeks divided between dry docks, silos,
and the yachts whose crews unwind noisily

beyond the founder's pious gaze –
his vision of strength graced by geometric streets,
palaces, the baroque churches
where believers sing praise to *Alla*.

Prickly Pear

A shabby and uncherishable growth,
it is at first unrecognised and scarcely noticed
as you make a roadside halt, your visitor's eye
lured by distant iconic vistas. And so,

inveigled always beyond the details,
you appraise each photo op, framing,
say, the Silent City raised up against the sky
on self-absorbed strategic heights;

or lose yourself in contemplation,
gazing through the Azure Window,
its accidental rock a masterpiece
shaped by the weather's bag of tricks –

a monument to impermanence
where, returning, you see at your feet
the evidence of countless tiny deaths
that went to form the island,

remembering, too, that the citadel
was built on fear. And later at the tourists'
market, jostled by crowds and trapped,
you sample the liquor of the prickly pear –

sweetish and pink, a shot of fire
laced with recognition, for now you'll see it
everywhere in spiked mittens
scrabbling over a drystone wall,

or the breeze block ruins of an outhouse.
Unprepossessing, thuggish,
it hoards its life and moisture in the fibrous
tangle of an impenetrable heart.

Mdina

As if it were a fist that has slowly opened
the Silent City draws you in –
as welcome as any stranger
to the quaint peace of its aftermath.

Past cabs whose horses idle, unfazed
by the notion of time, you cross
a bridge that spans the disused moat,
where now a lemon grove

rolls out its spangled carpet.
The fault-lines of creedal war
have shifted since to bleaker zones,
yet here, through clenched centuries,

the conflict was defined where,
on its still imposing gateway
the pagan is memorialised
who accepted grace and shared his roof

with a shipwrecked apostle.
Renamed by each invader,
it returned at last by quiet declension
to the semitic of its native tongue.

Only the great and good
can afford to live here now
– grandees and a few contemplatives –
rumoured presences behind high walls

that cast their cooling shadows
down crooked streets and alleyways –
a genteel maze designed
to impede an arrow's flight.

Malti

A salt-hardened vernacular fetched
from who knows where by raiders,
their sights fixed on the main chance –

or a language as sedimentary
as the islands where it thrives,
the impacted layers of influence

bringing forth a growth
that's tough as the prickly pear
and bloody-mindedly

survives diaspora –
recalling the words
of Joseph, our guide,

who had made his stash in Australia:
*Sure, we all know English,
but I couldn't speak it to my sons.*

And, as each semitic day
begins or ends with Roman greetings:
bonġu, bonswa,

a language hinting
at reconciliation: like Aristotle
absorbed by Ibn Sina.

Maltese Buses

For a couple of coins that otherwise
might disappear mysteriously
into the fluff of your pocket
you'll get where you want on the island,
if you have time to spare.

The drivers are a closed book,
or are bound by a vow of silence.
Understanding your language,
they know that theirs
is one you'll never learn.

Their seat is a sacred space
in 1950s buses, decked out
like wayside shrines.
A Virgin sanctions disregard
for their own *No Smoking* signs.

The routes they follow take you
past ubiquitous churches.
With a clock set right
and another wrong, the faithful
confound simple-minded devils.

III. When Smokey Sings

Bookshop

I was still involved in the world
of nature when, aged twelve or so,
I first climbed its wonky staircase,
ascending step by creaking step
from what was new and 'now'
to bays of books with history.

Their inked inscriptions,
leached to rusty shades of brown,
enshrined the names of previous owners.
They had scuffed boards and faded
titles, or wrappers frayed and torn,
the imprimatur of frequent use.

With scant means, I browsed
for hours the teeming plates
in field guides, absorbing
their poetry of genera and species,
and loved the way *Observer's* books
perched in the palm of a hand.

Over time I moved on,
exploring different fields of study
in the colour-coded volumes
of *Everyman* hardback classics,
or resurrecting live poets
from dusty shelves of duffers.

Home again from university,
I learned how everything
had gone in flames and pictured
books they'd dumped in skips –
their spatchcocked spines and smoked
pages, their reek of desolation.

When Smokey Sings

To get past the door to the Top Rank
disco every Saturday afternoon
you needed a suit, so mine
was a lifeless grey, a cast-off,
with narrow lapels that even then
I knew had never been fashionable.

Once in you were lost to darkness,
until your eyes adjusted,
bumping around the outer tables,
where you searched for mates
who talked big and smoked,
nursing Pepsi Colas.

In class we had learned
from Brother Vergilius, confused
and sheepish as we were,
about the risks involved in kissing,
how one thing might lead
to another, but somehow never did.

In the end the music got you
– Muscle Shoals, the Motor City –
making moves in a circle
next to a circle of girls.
Above it all the mirror ball
became your ruling planet.

Stepping Out

Sumer is icumen in.
Anon. Reading Abbey

Clapton is God!
Anon. Various walls

My new look that summer
was vagrant chic:
a stylized take
on Wurzel Gummidge
that had me sweltering
in a trench coat
and battered
trilby hat,
my washed-to-rags
T-shirts finished off
flamboyantly
with a red bandana
tied around my neck.

In the Age of Peel
and Woodstock
altered rites
prevailed as music
filled the cloisters
I had paced
on church parades –
white boys
wailing blues
where late
the sweet birds sang.

Gasometers

I never understood how they functioned or why,
but a single gasometer beside the canal
brings back childhood. Leaning against
the railings, I see beneath me
the same swans drag their murky reflections.

Yet thinking back, there may have been more,
where now the concrete apron holds out
forlornly against rough grass and buddleia–
a listless space that might be healed
by the uncertain touch of money.

With a head for heights and a vision
I could be drawn to clouds up ladders
or go sky-walking around its rim.
Grounded, I see a stark geometry, the grace
acquired when things outlive their use;

amazed, too, by the thought of how
contraptions so huge and intricate can
be dismantled and then just carted away.
Like harmoniums breathing stiffly,
I imagined them wheezing up and down.

Each time I passed the levels were different,
even if, like time, I never saw them move.
It seems that years are slow seepage.
They are colourless, odourless, tasteless,
as in some definition I once learned at school.

Oscar Wilde Walk, Reading

A rain-darkened gallery
of colonnaded trees,
it's hemmed in
on one side by brickwork,
opening out on the other
to a refurbished
view of water,
along which
commissioned railings
spell out their faith
in Wilde's *beautiful world* –
a perfectability
embodied
here in civic pride.

Though summer
again seems touch and go,
a *flâneur* might pause
between the showers
to take his ease
in a love seat,
watching a narrow boat
that barely makes it
beneath the bridge,
as if it were slipping
through the eye
of a needle
or the darker
passage to Hades.

For Antoinette

On a wet afternoon in Wetherspoon's
I came across her, gazing intently,
like a survivor from some *belle époque*,
into the mirror of her make-up box;
and making herself presentable
for a night out and its chances,
she applied eye shadow and liner
with a practised hand, then blended
a blusher to the natural tint of her skin.
From time to time she paused,
deflating the banter, risqué and obvious,
of daytime regulars in a drawl
as rich as poured molasses.
She said her name was Antoinette –
mixed race, Belizean, and proud
of genes that shaped her cheek bones,
her hair as sleek as Jeanne Duval's
and which she brushed and brushed,
her rhythm slow, insistent.

IV. A Murmuration

A Murmuration

Something is gathering
at the edge of the evening,

a shoaling of consciousness
as light fails,

each speck a singularity,
an occurrence of will,

as the living skein is formed
to twist and glimmer

like a burnt-out image
of the Northern Lights.

One by one,
they'll come to roost

in a city of leaves,
a settlement of feathers.

A Northern Resort

for Phyll Smyth

That tacky parade of gift shops,
amusements, and cheap cafés,
touting for Sunday strollers,
confronts an expanse of winter sea

with a chirpy faith
in its permanence: a structure
raised in an age of cagey virtues
as a pleasure-ground for low pay.

When the first trains
clattered in, a skylight opened up
in the miners' vaulted dark;
and straight-laced locals

staked a claim
in gifts accrued from Progress:
a pier and a neat stone prom
giving shape to a coast

that drifts, a definition
so that work might leave its mark.
But summers here were duds,
and money seeks a florid climate.

A baroque of shells and gimcrack
won't bring those heydays back –
their awkward smiles
staring from faded snaps.

The Owls of Cleethorpes

i.m. Nelson Mandela

No one knows how long the owls
had spent inside the trees,
reviled at first then trapped
by the god of grudges.
Hooped in rings of growth,
a drizzle of sap sustained them
through the creaking dark.

When strangers came
with bags of tools they set to
and lopped the branches,
silencing their canopies.

They made each trunk
a pedestal, chiselling free
the birds until, larger
than life and monumental,
they shook off at last
their wooden feathers.

To the Lighthouse

To make it out to the lighthouse
you'll first unravel the headland road
as it winds round a boardwalk
pounded by the beautiful
who power walk or jog
beneath a peerless sky then past
the villas peeking coyly
through subtropical leaves.

And when you've arrived
as far east as roads can take you,
park up beneath the outcrop
of Wollumbin or Mount Warning,
sacred still to men who've won
the right, belatedly, to trundle
barrows of sand and stone
up and down its pathway.

You, too, will make the ascent,
skirting unnameable growth
and a wind-sculpted tree,
until, dazed by distances,
above your head you'll see it,
bone-white, transcendent,
asserting benignly its own
claim to permanence.

With its eight tons of prism
afloat in a pool of mercury
it smashes sun to fragments
each afternoon when
the angle's right. In the dark
it's an oracle, revealing
only the certainties
of white fellas who built it.

Koala

Adrift on tides of sluggishness,
but awakened now and then
by faint pangs of hunger,
its pulse is a distant rumour
muffled deep in fur.

In the dreamtime what possessed it
to plump for leaves of eucalyptus?
– when what they are is mostly
water with fuel enough to reach
another and then another,

until the creature's islanded
in a roadside windbreak
or some farmer's modest yard –
beyond which lies the emptiness
we admire as scenery,

making our way in a hired car
past the neat plantations,
the pasturelands, the cleared
slopes of panoramas
that take your breath away.

Leaving St. Kilda

The philanthropists
found them a better place.
On the day they left
they kept their fires lit,
and laid out oats
for their cross-grained *lares*.
The text that day
was *Exodus*.

When they bumped ashore
on a different coast,
their home was a perch
for the fulmar and gannet.

So let their lament
be the song of extremes:
a liturgical shriek of gulls,
the high wind's *missa solemnis*.

Ontology

On Cleethorpes beach the tide is out,
where gulls dispute their stretch
of puddled sand: a paradigm to taunt me
as they snatch what gain they can,
their broken cries a colloquy
that's tough and unforgiving, while
against each blast that freights them
I hug my collar closer. Optimism –
it's a string of toy-town lights,
painted bulbs that vie
with the elements' big effects.

Stéphane Mallarmé

A hapless pedagogue shunted between
provincial towns and hoodwinked Heads,

you absent-mindedly lost your pupils
in the wilderness of *Lear*.

Bone-weary, definitively bored,
you failed to impart so much as a word

of purely functional English, fluent only
in the poetry of Edgar Allen Poe.

For years you wangled paid leave
or survived on family hand-outs,

whittling away an inheritance
your early demise made sure

you'd never need, when finally
the Mistral destroyed you.

What mattered were rumours of greatness
that lay behind intractable pages –

your desolate quest for an absolute
in the glacial lake of verse.

Sea Breeze

Mallarmé

The flesh is weary. And books, I've read them all.
To fly away, escape, somewhere, like a bird
that's high in the rush of spray and foreign skies.
What's to keep me here? Nothing! Not the grace
of formal gardens that once assuaged the eye,
when now the oppressed spirit seeks its sea-change –
not nights when the desolate glare of a lamp
is reflected in the blank impenetrable page,
not even the mother nursing my child.
And so away! The creaking masts are calling.
Weigh anchor for hallucinatory lands.

Mortal tedium, so often deceived by hopes,
needs to believe in the handkerchiefs waving
their last goodbyes, though bound perhaps for shipwreck
I may be lost at sea, and far from fragrant islands –
But, O my heart, hear how the sailors sing!

August Schleicher

The shades of an *Urwelt* haunted each thought,
the scholarly psyche possessed. Across
that vague arena he sensed a people moving,
could feel like a pulse the groundswell

of history, its rhythms of violence,
settlement, rights: a landscape of voices –
for language, too, was a part of that flux,
a cacophony where he sought order.

The summers he spent in Lithuania
he worked with the dead on forgotten farms,
and heard in songs how the vowels rang though
like bells. Only he transcribed them,

though his fieldwork wasn't enough.
When he wrote his fable, *The Sheep and Horses*,
his primal text was a flower
from the seedbed of flexion and lexis.

The Swan

Rilke

Making our way laboriously through lists
of things to do, complexities that ensnare us,
we are like the shambling swan –

until, dying, we lose all purchase
on terra firma, slipping away like the swan,
as he settles, at first uncertainly,

into the water that buoys him
and flows on blithely in endless ripples,
while he, so still and self-assured

in the achievement
of majesty, deigns to drift,
untrammelled, where the current takes him.

The Pheasant

A small time hustler, a princeling,
he's on the make and mooching
down along the hedgerows.

His head in the cloud
of each moment's business,
the world is lying at its feet.

On a whim, his thoughts
a-scamper, he sets off
on a pointless dash

from one place to another
then remembers flight.
Climbing raucously

above the stubble,
his song's in the key
of twisting metal.

And when the time's right
his sex is functional.
It's all him, his pageantry –

for any drab will do.
Inheriting robes
from distant Asia

does he dream of lives
he's bred for, or guess
how it will end

here at the roadside
– cast off by
a casual bumper,

his gauds in disarray,
his dark flesh ripening
beneath a perfect sky?

The Hunters in the Snow

They are returning home across the snow,
three men and their dogs, who may have set out
early. Shouldering poles, they make their way
past the people who are tending a fire.
Unaware of the details my eyes seek,
they move on slowly through derelict trees.

Hunched silhouettes, their faces are hidden,
yet smart in a wind that flattens the flames.
Above their heads the network of branches
has unravelled to a pattern of nerves
rubbed raw in deadening cold. At their heels
a skinny pack slouches towards its straw.

The famished landscape expands beyond them
where they hear, perhaps, the cries of skaters
ferried across through a chilly distance.
The figures below, excited, breathless,
are unconcerned with the ultimate plan –
my abstract joy in a clear perspective.

Imperceptibly daylight fades away
as birds come down to roost. My eye sweeps up
to salient peaks that now, like some fort
abandoned, are holding out in a waste
of sky; and there only a magpie flies,
viewing the scene that Bruegel invented.

Two Rivers Press has been publishing in and about Reading since 1994. Founded by the artist Peter Hay (1951–2003), the press continues to delight readers, local and further afield, with its varied list of individually designed, thought-provoking books.